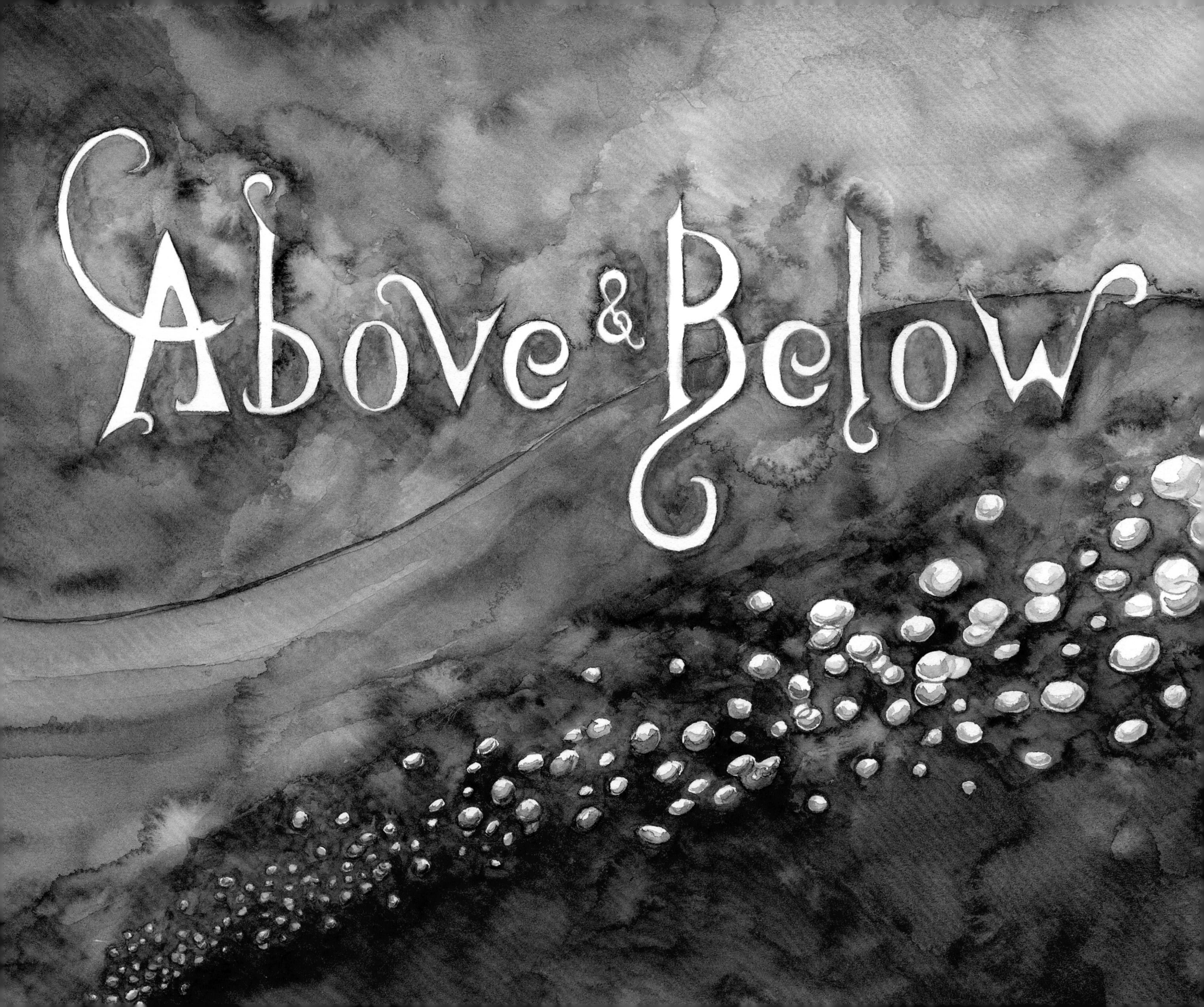
Above & Below

The Voyages of Virgilio

Mia Wolff

Fantagraphics Underground Seattle, Washington

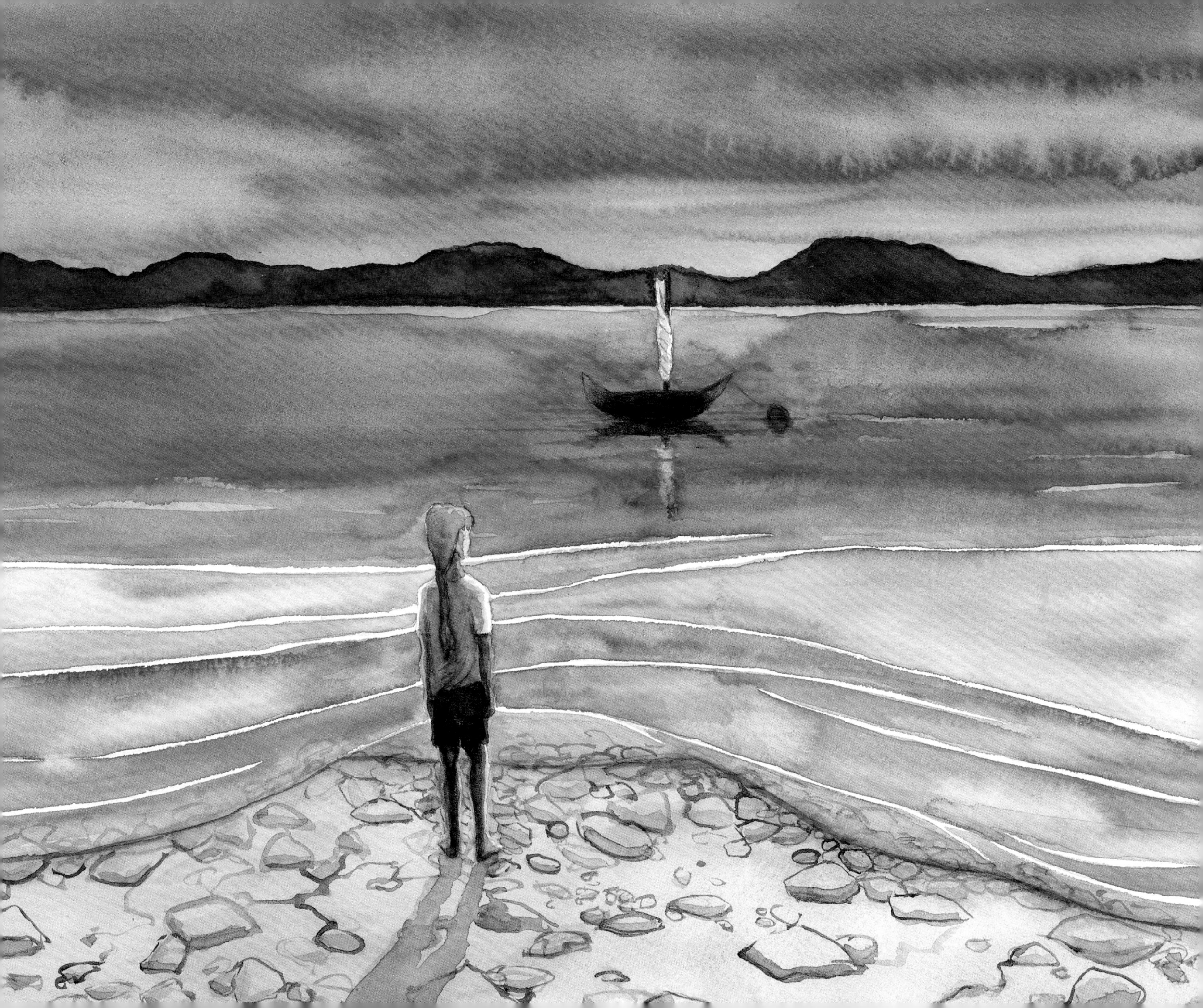

Virgilio loved the water

He was a wonderful swimmer

On a silvery dreamlike night

Waves whispered and stars glistened

As he swam to his ship in the river

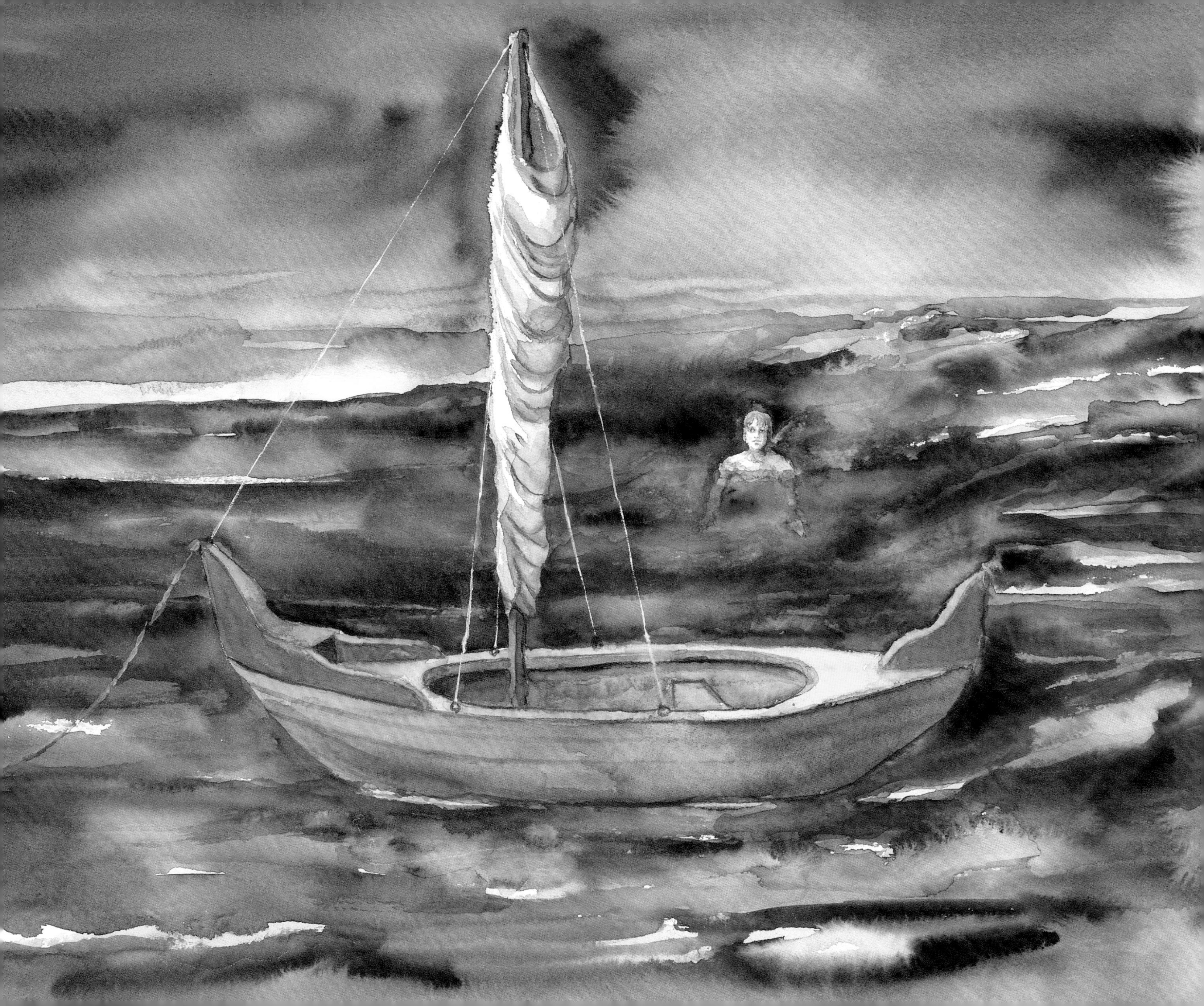

Above were Venus and Mars

And a thousand stars

Along with the tide he went

Below the eels dreamt

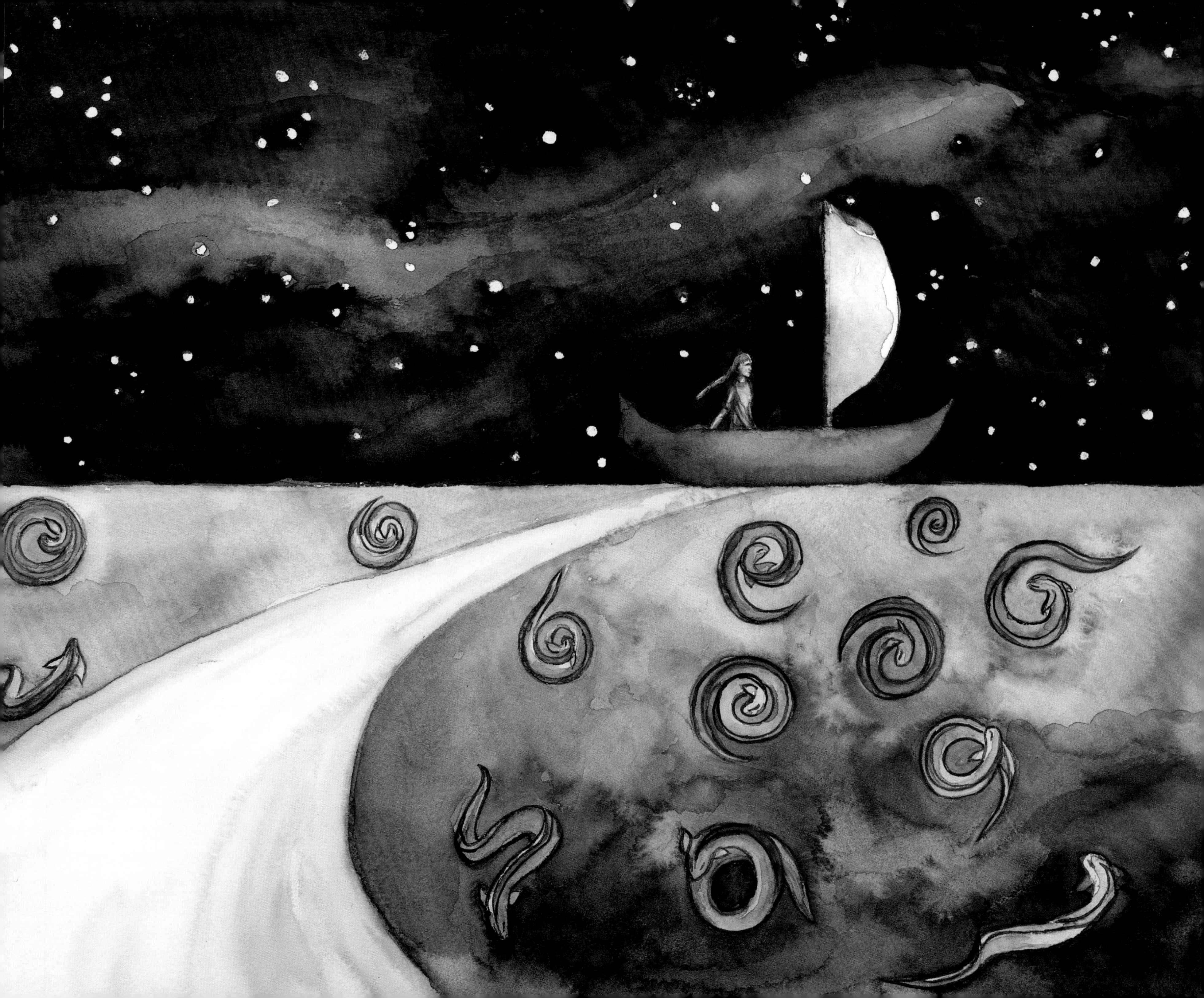

Sail wide and current swift

He chased the moon down river drift

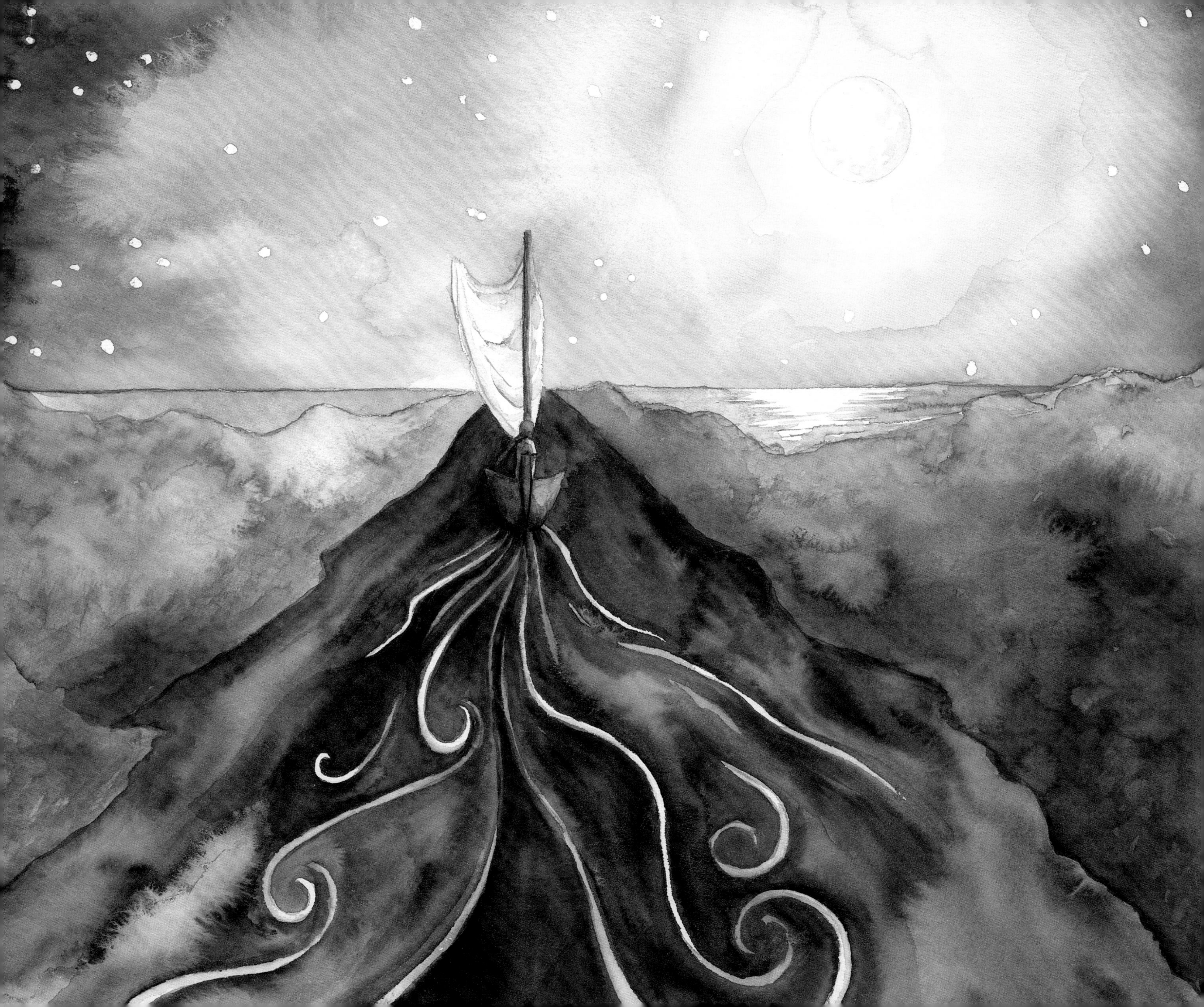

Past the city and lady he sailed

Above the sky melted rainbows

Below the river was veiled

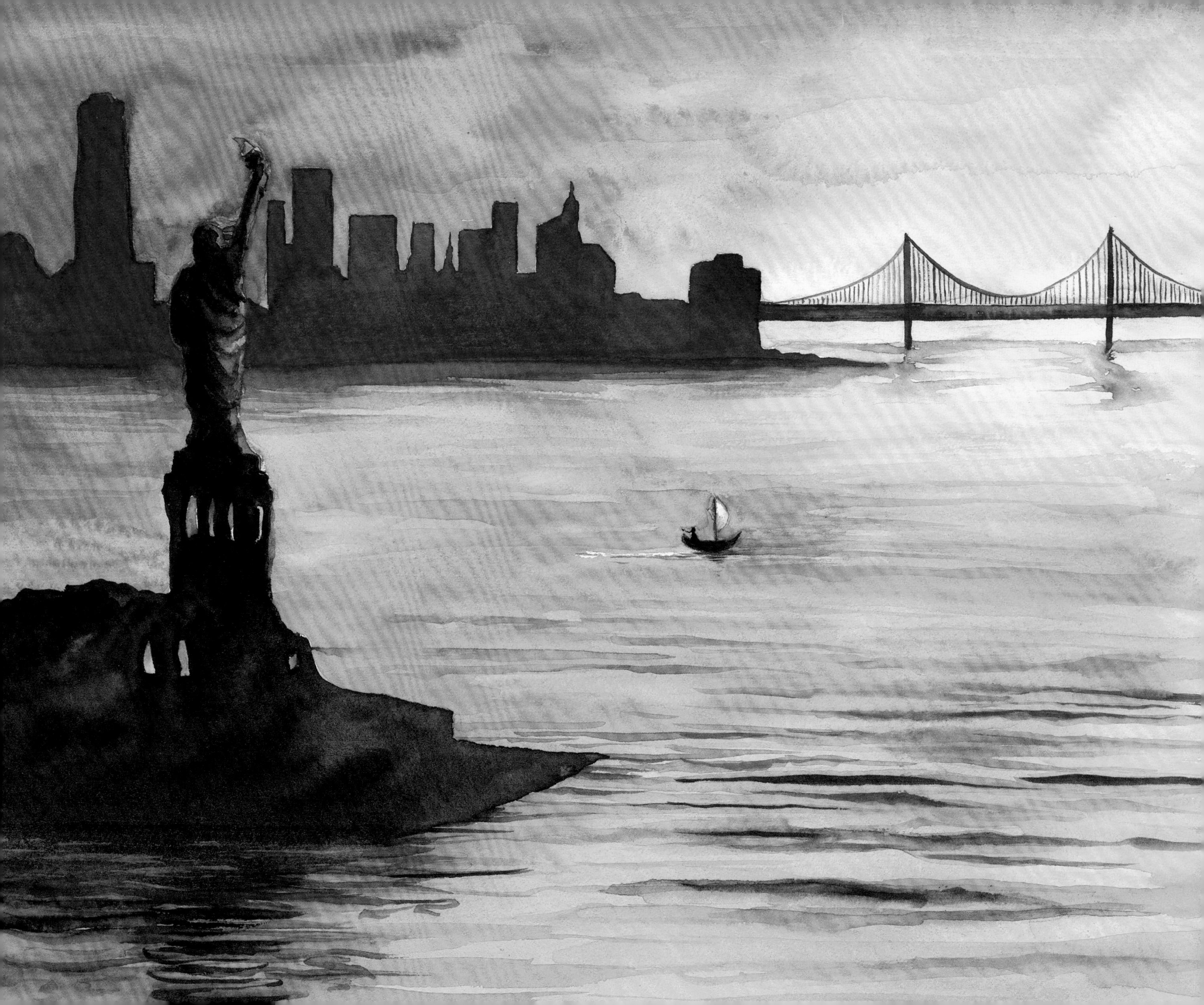

Toward the sun he sailed into change

Above the sky was clear

Below the sea was strange

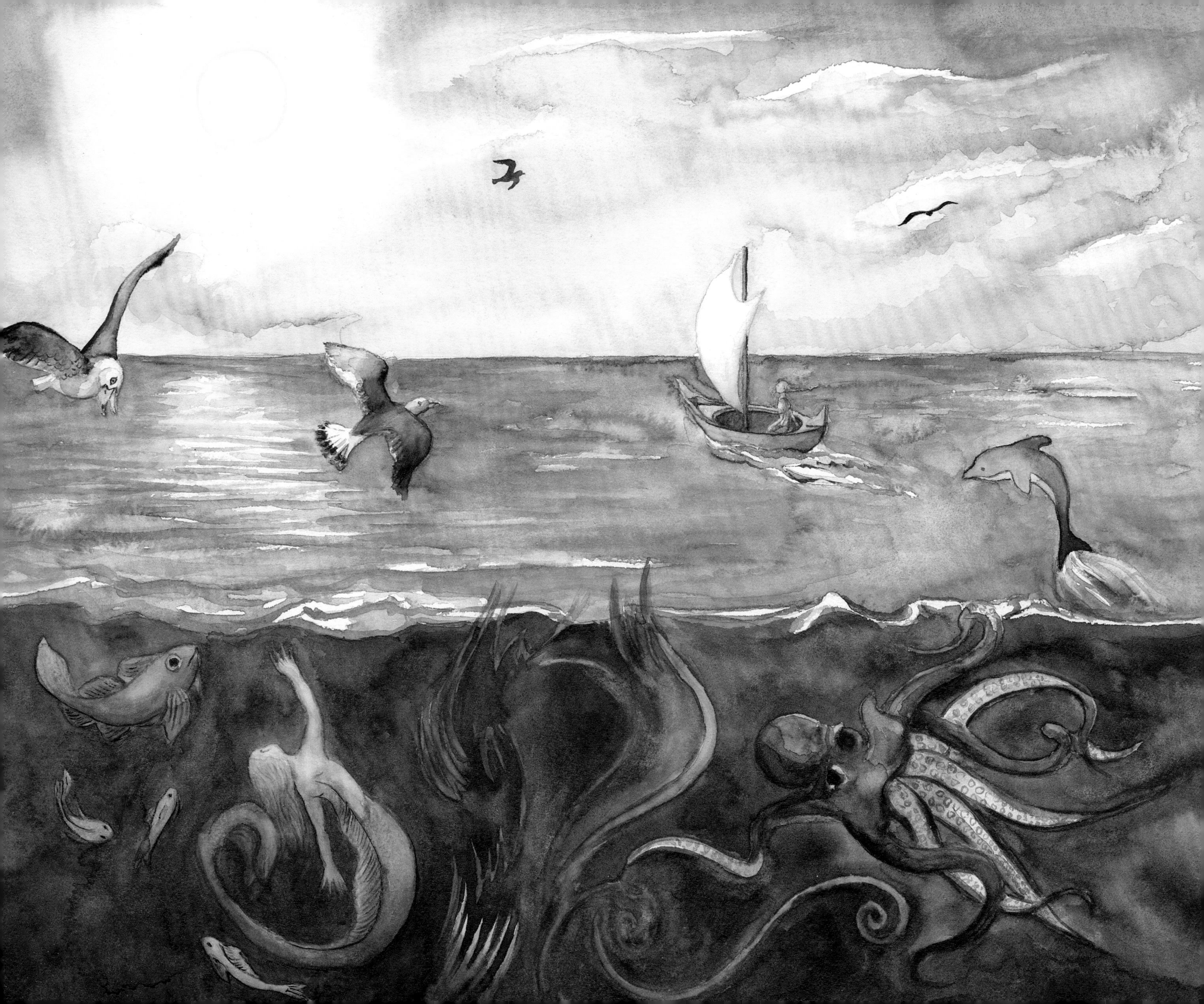

With soot stained clouds a storm came

Lifting the sea and rending the sky

Above dragons sizzled in the rain

Below wars raged and soldiers died

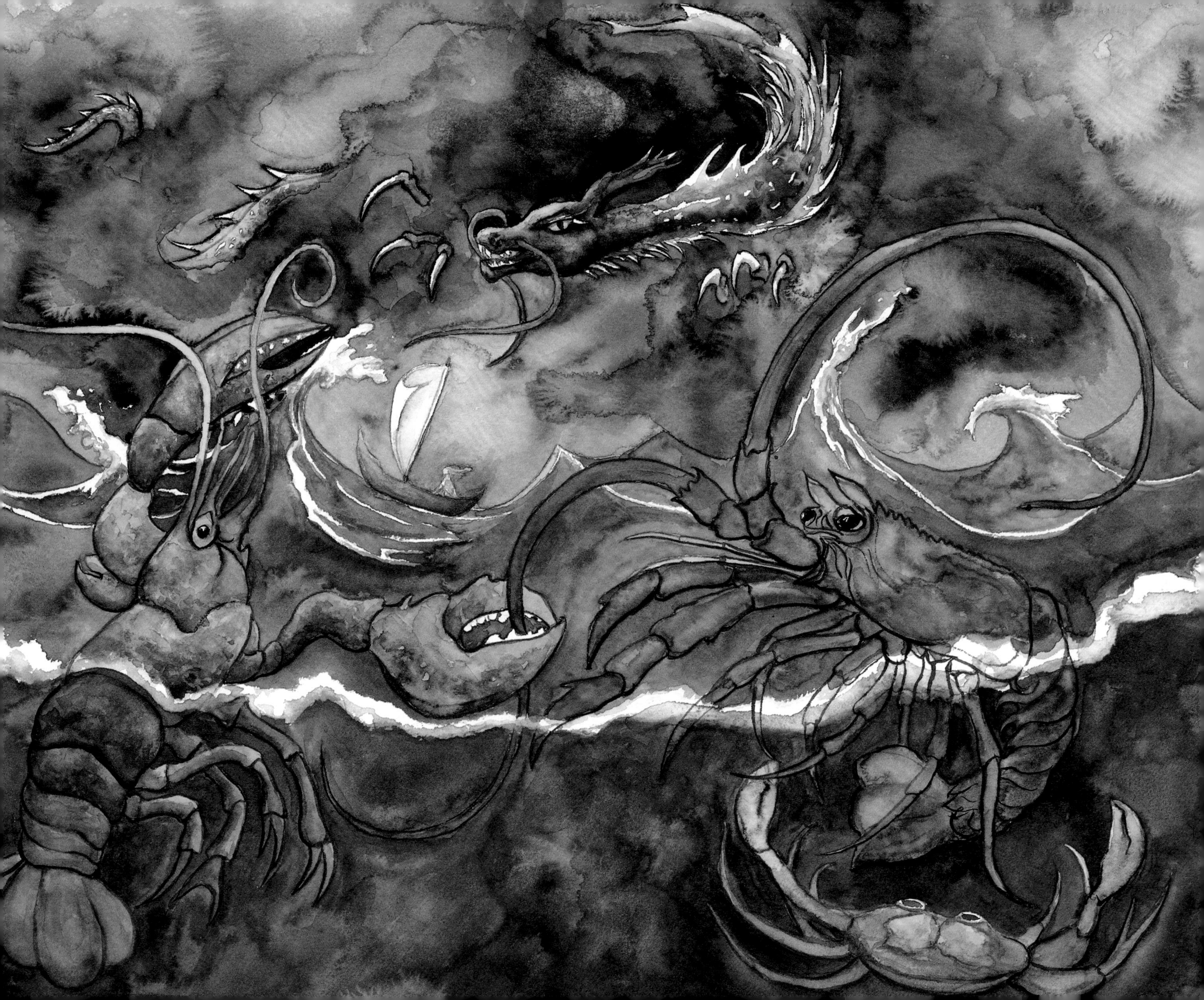

Waves parted and Virgilio's ship
Swung over their dark and foaming lip

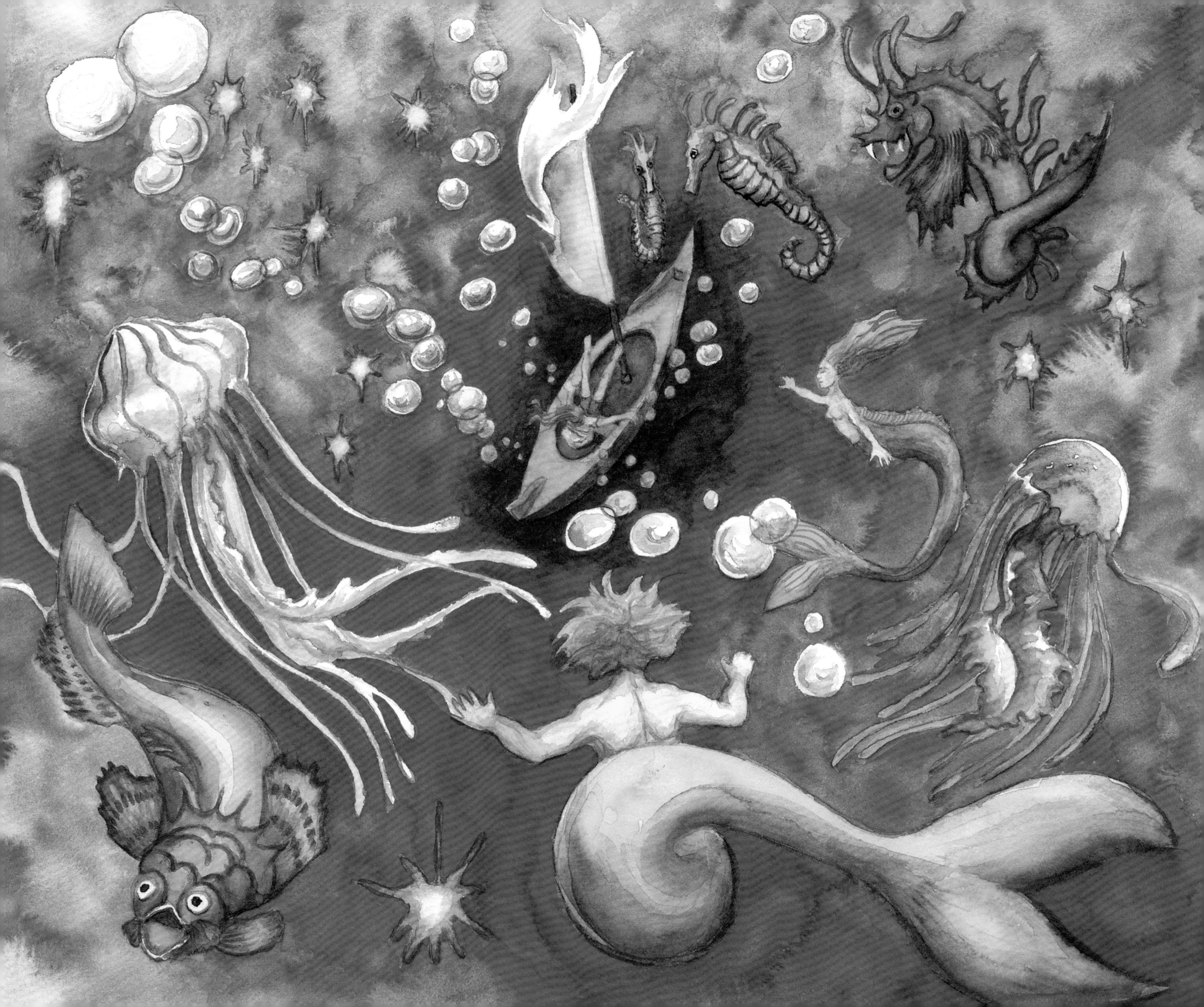

As his ship sank, flying in sleep

He floated off into the deep

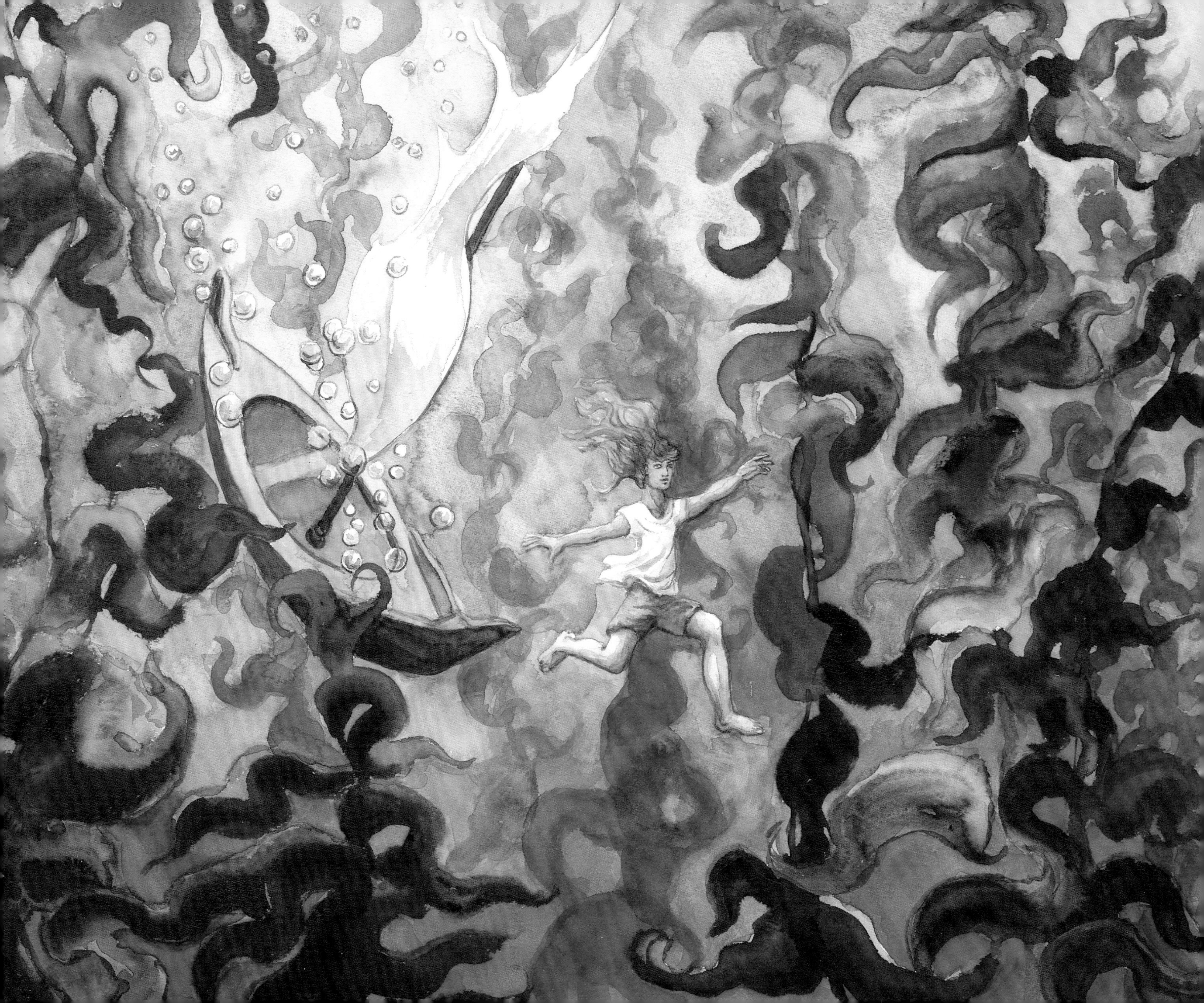

Hung in the seaweed: rubies and pearls

Skeletons circled around his head

There at the bottom of the world

Virgilio danced with the dead

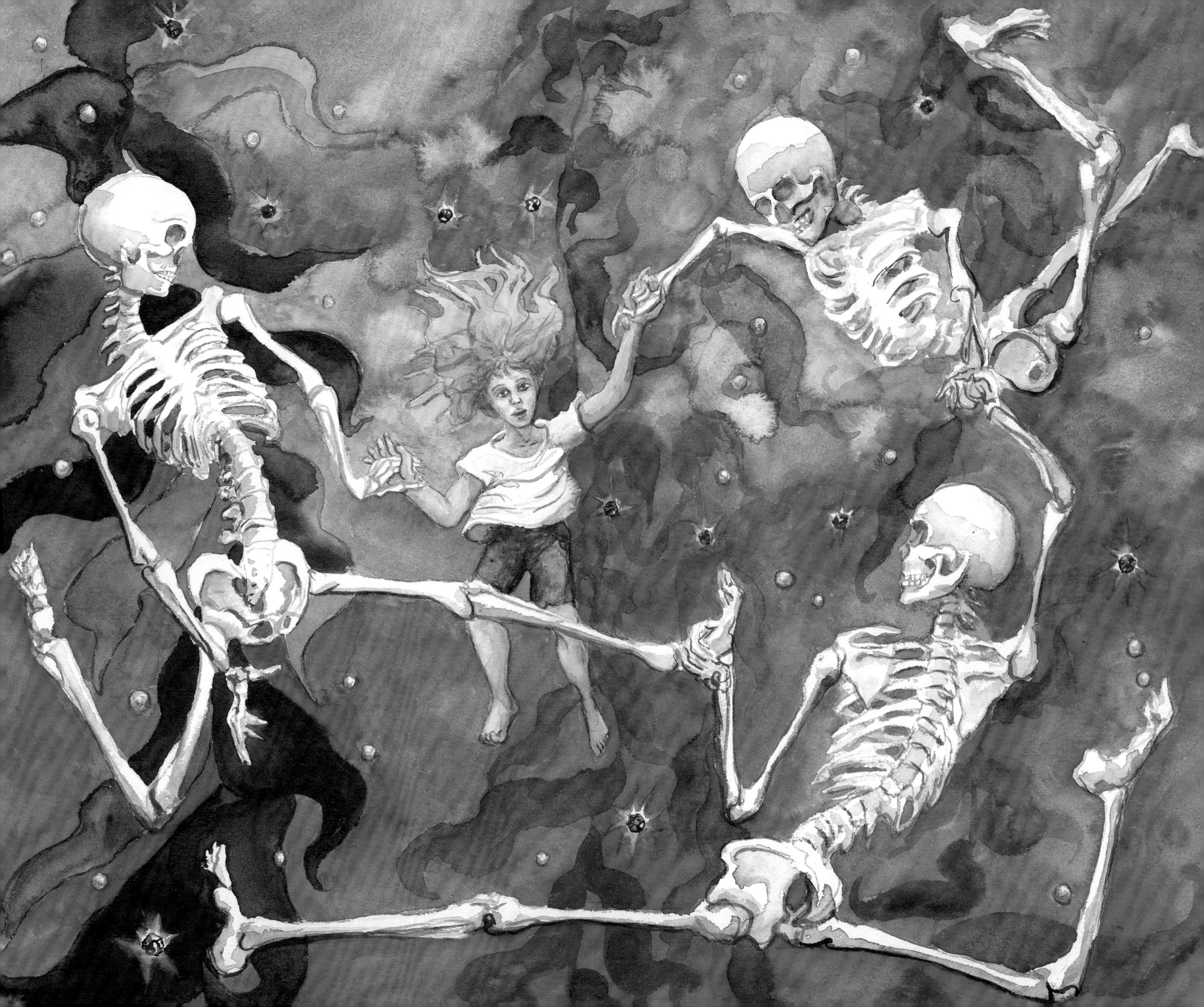

Below a valley of violet night —

Above their lonely dance

Fell dawn's jeweled light —

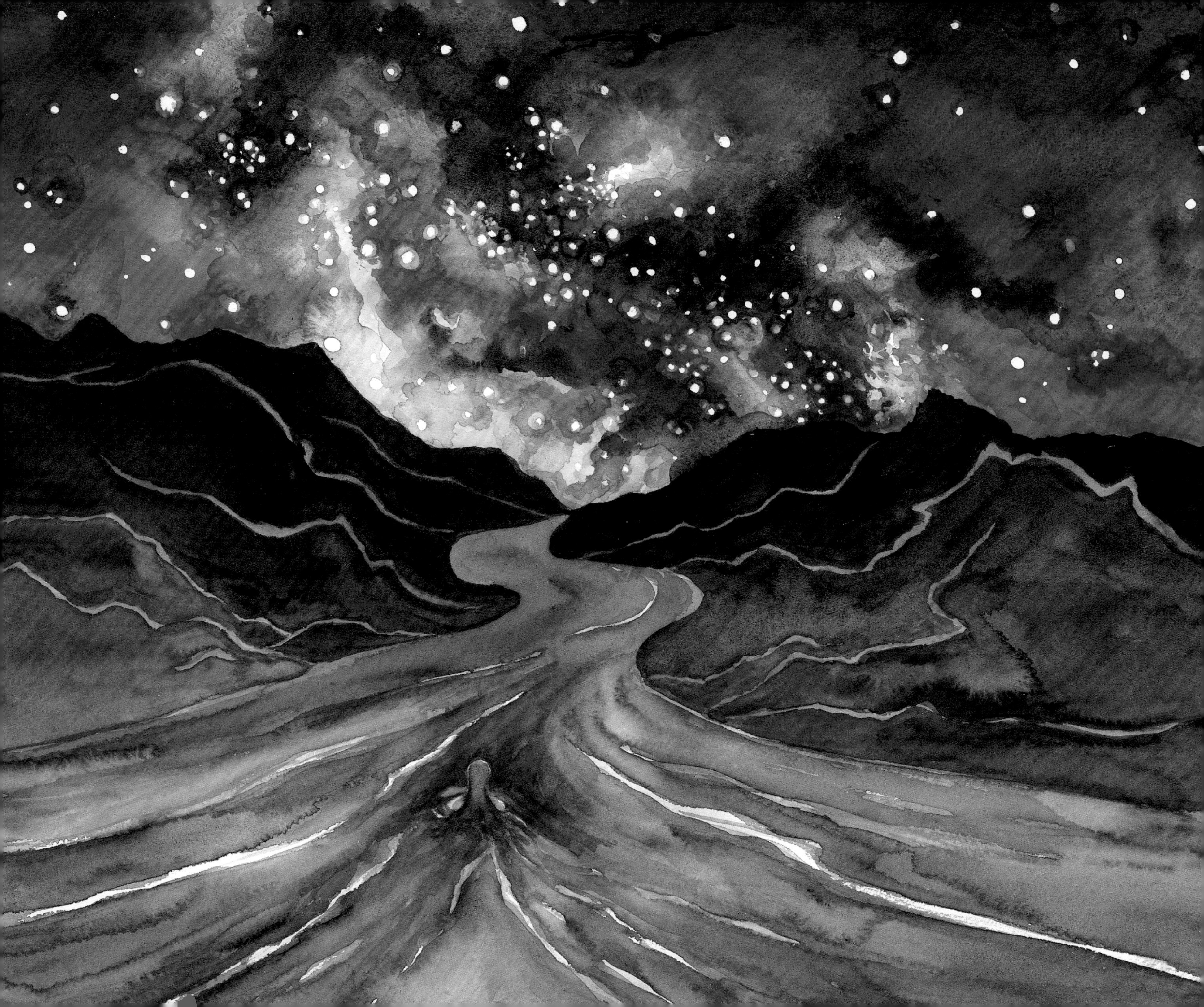

Mia Wolff is a painter who also makes books. She went from art school to the circus and then back to New York and painting. She did a lot of martial arts and worked as a masseuse and Pilates trainer as well as teaching trapeze. She has a great fascination with words and pictures. She painted and wrote a children's book, *Catcher*, and collaborated with Samuel R Delany on the graphic novel *Bread & Wine*. She also has a mad hobby of studying Chinese. She lives in Brooklyn.

Editor: Gary Groth
Design: Justin Allan-Spencer and Mia Wolff
Associate Publisher: Eric Reynolds
Publisher: Gary Groth

Above and Below: The Voyages of Virgilio is
copyright © 2022 Mia Wolff.
All rights reserved. All permission to
reproduce content must be obtained in
writing from the publisher.

FANTAGRAPHICS UNDERGROUND

F.U. Press is an imprint of Fantagraphics Books Inc.
7563 Lake City Way NE, Seattle, WA 98115
fantagraphics.com/fu

ISBN: 978-1-68396-547-3
First printing: January 2022. Printed in China
FU053

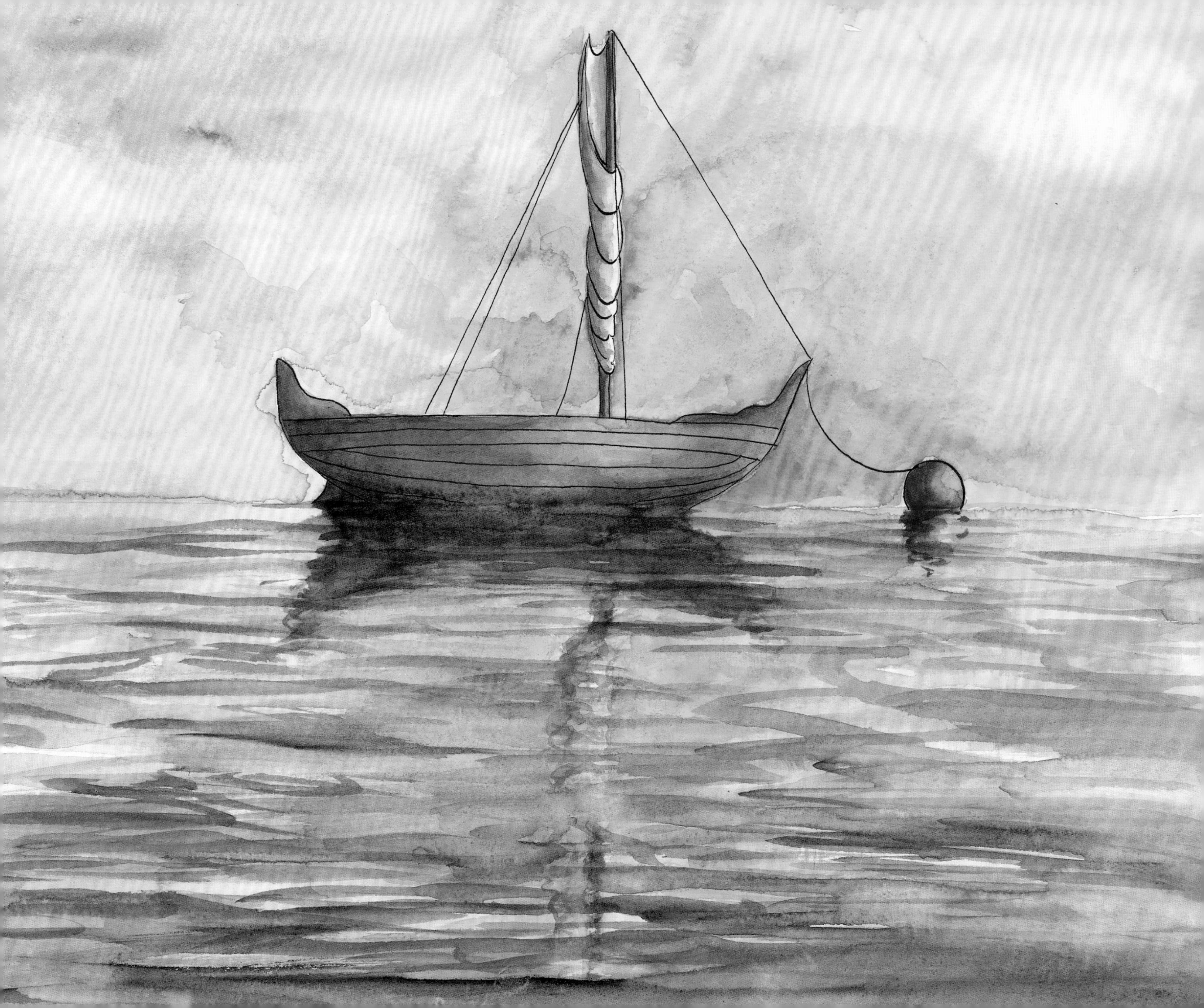

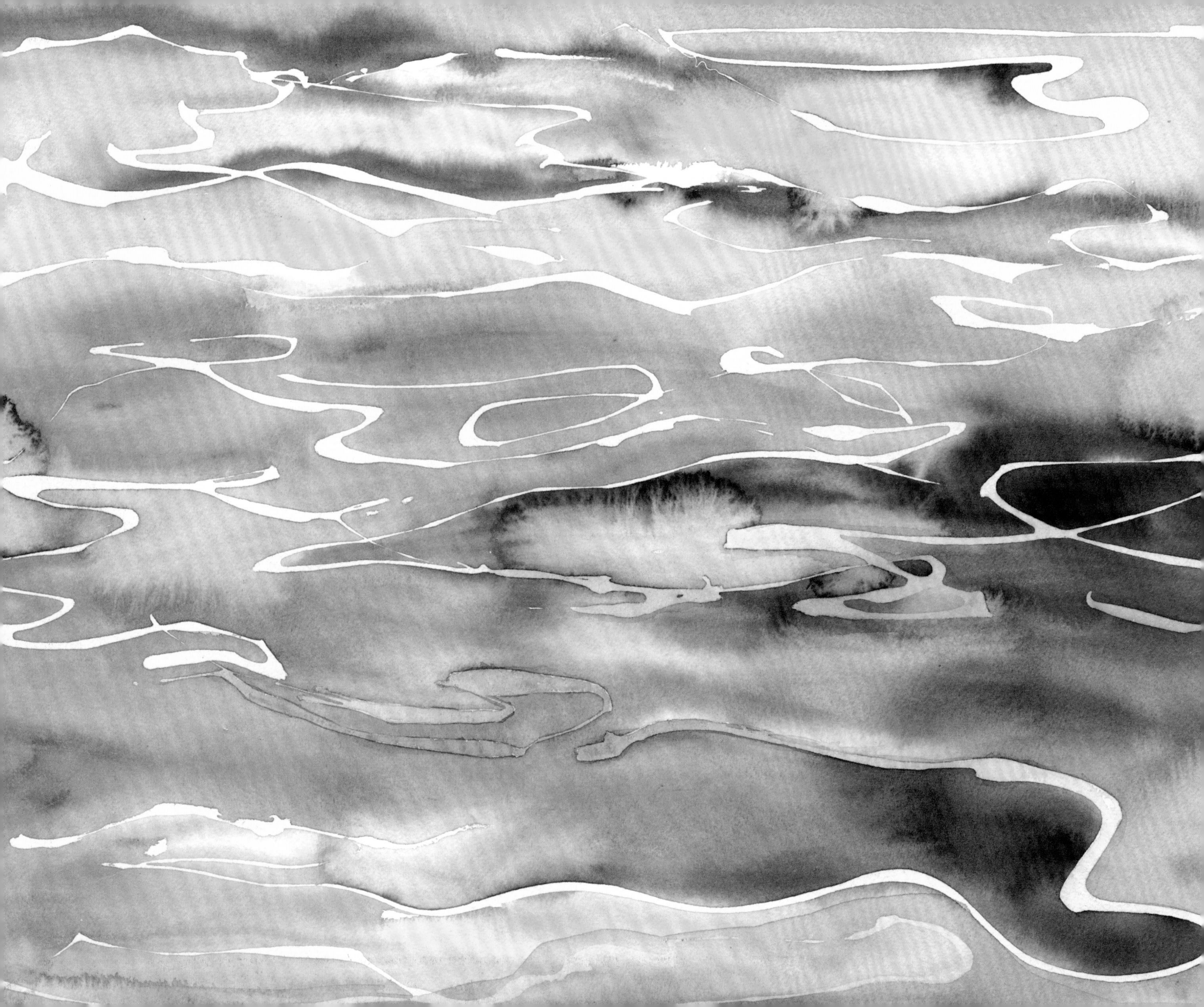